I'm Not a Mourning Person

Sarah Kenney

BookLeaf Publishing

India | USA | UK

Presentation by *BookLeaf Publishing*

Web: www.bookleafpub.com

E-mail: info@bookleafpub.com

ISBN: 9789358736564

First edition 2023

*For all those who have supported me and
my writing through the ages, thanks for
letting me scribble on napkins and send you
sad stuff all the time. All My Love.*

*For all those that I've lost, who inspired
and continue to inspire me in spirit—I love
and miss you dearly.*

*For all those who are reading, may your
own journey lead you just where you need
to be.*

Cheetah Print Coat

Take off your Cheetah Print Coat,
leave your boots at the door,
come here just a little bit closer, I'd like to hold
you once more
Time is working against us
As we sit in the waiting room, by the ICU door
We aren't here long before, Life is declared no
more
We gather our things, unsure what to say, a
young dear life has been lost today.
your coat still remains hanging on the rack,
as a beacon of warm light, as a sign to not look
back
as a symbol of your rarity, standing out against
the pack
a solemn reminder of the day our hearts turned
black.
In this extreme grief we say goodbye,
My, how lives shatter when a young one dies.

Funeral

Every funeral attended prior
had been of old age
watching them lay the old soul finally to rest
in the stained wooden boxes surrounded by
family
This one is different
In no way was I prepared
to see your ageless face in
this lifeless box to be carried
       away,
away from those who called you names,
I'm sorry honey,
away from your family,
they loved you so,
away from your friends and school,
There is no escape of,
never knowing the joys of what could
have been.
As I watch you carried away,
      away
      in death's black box.

Catelya

I'm missing you today
It happens all the time
The sadness comes in waves
Even though I seem fine

You were called too soon
We weren't ready for you to die
I'm thankful for the time that was given
And the chance to say goodbye

Sometimes this life gets hard
Even seems I'm at my end
I wouldn't change it for the world
For life would be very different

You're the reason I am who I am
I can't thank you enough for that
But the sole thing I want the most of all
Is for God to give you back.

Anxiety

It cuts like a knife, not a sharp one.
No, it hits its target and weighs me
                              Down.

                              Inching ever lower,
slowly.
It hurts and I feel trapped
I am trapped, I always am
While my brain screams nasty things over and
over
I breathe heavily, hard and fast
The tears have started
Why does the mind torture me so?
The minutes pass as I recollect myself
Attempting to fit unmatched puzzle pieces
Into place for just a little while,
Hoping that I do not shatter again today.

Xanax

5

The storm has come
And so has the pain
Take the blue pill, you won't feel a thing
The crying will stop
The brain will cease
The little blue pills are quick release
Before you know it the mind has stopped,
You're gritting your teeth; You're going numb
It's easy to sleep, forget all your pain
Take the blue pill, you won't feel a thing

Funeral II

I've been here before,
But now,
I've seen enough ageless faces in boxes to be
considered "professional" at this
I never really considered the box idea, until you,
when I came face to face with your box.
I saw your box as I stood in the center of an altar
way
Frozen
Panicked
Not a normal type of panic, just straight
trepidation.
I wonder if it's the same feeling Pandora had,
when she first laid eyes on her box.
The rallying of a thousand different outcomes
fated by one stupid miscalculation,
yet the overwhelming and desperate desire, NO
MATTER WHAT----
to see what is in the box.
I wanted to know what was in your box.
Certainly, it couldn't have been you.
I mean, shit
We'd need one box just for your humor,
Another for your heart,
Surely, that had to be too big for that box

Had I miscalculated?
The entirety of one human's life,
Love,
Connection,
Couldn't fit in a box.
For a moment, I felt a deep sense of anger
Then I realized we were all suffering a dilemma,
this wasn't Pandora's Box.
It was Schrodinger's.
Where the contents are both simultaneously
alive and dead.
There you were liminal,
Alive in the tears being shed by your friends,
By your mother and sister's unrequited love,
By the stories we told around a burning chair
your punk-ass broke,
In a really nice, cold, Mexican lager
In a sublime song.
Such is the paradox of grief,
that it is simultaneously world-ending and
life-enchanting.

Anxiety II

I think, I think,
Until I overthink
and the thought is distorted and bad.
I think, I think,
of all good things, until anxiety turns them bad.
One minute you're here,
the next you're gone,
My heart just wants you to stay
I think, I think,
this is a convoluted mind game we play.
I am the pawn, not the Queen
in this ultimate game of chess,
All I do is move
the spaces and hope I am the best.
It's hard to play, this game is old,
All efforts have been put to the test.
For it's not a fair game, all that I play,
Anxiety plays me best.

First Lady Lazarus

I met the First Lady Lazarus
My dear friend, Emily
We sat and talked of many things,
Death & Immortality.

A Taste of Liquor Never Brewed,
How hope's a fleeting thing,
The constant beating in my head—
The Funeral in my Brain.

She told me her life had stood a loaded gun,
I said I understood
For it seems we both have courted death,
Hoping to meet him in the Wood.

To feel the pain—so utter
To go safely, with an open eye
I met the First Lady Lazarus,
She taught me how to die.

Therapy

Got fucked up again,
My favorite, unwanted, friend
Stumbled and landed in therapy,
Now, here I sit eating packages of mints
While a stranger spiels on how to take care of
"me".

Mantra

Mantra, Mantra
Just beat into my head
Think positive affirmations,
Forget the existential dread

How stupid I must look,
Just talking to myself
Repeating all these words
While my mind stirs somewhere else

Mantra, Mantra
Just beat it into my head
Think positive affirmations
While all my friends are dead

Going one hundred miles a minute,
The clock it doesn't stop,
Sit back and count the seconds,
Listen to the tick-tock

Mantra, Mantra
Just beat it into my head
Think positive affirmations
then crawl back into bed.

Apology Letter From My Brain to My Heart

I wish you knew how incredibly frustrating you
are—
The rational thoughts turned more intuition
Following what's right, logical or not—
But this isn't about gut feeling
Refereeing to settle our score—

I just want you to know that while we may
disagree,
You are still the Heart to my Brain; we are one.
Unified in body, unified in life, though separate
in thought.

An intricate network designed to support one
another,
With unique intelligence to ourselves.
I know you can feel me,
As I feel you.
So let's remember we're in this together,
For the best and the worst of it.

Grief Is a Glitterbomb

Grief is a Glitterbomb
Strung about the floor—
I keep vacuuming it up,
But then I find more.

I think that it's gone
And I've cleaned all the places
Yet, still glitter appears
In the smallest of spaces.

From a corner of my mind, that I shut in the dark
A Birthday, A Song,
A Book, Works of Art
Like it was yesterday, and it falls just like rain
It is sweet, it is bitter,
but it's still glitter all the same.

Autumn

Autumn winds begin to blow,
Colored leaves, fall fast and slow,
Whirling, Twirling, All-Around,
Until at last, they touch the ground—

The tree, once golden, now dies,
A ritualistic dance of goodbye,
As the veins of life, run dry.

While the falling leaves
Utter their last prayers
To a rising Twilight Sky.

One day soon, I too shall fall,
Faded, Dry, Spoiled-all,
And as the season slowly creeps,
I cannot help but feel one with leaves.

Frail and crushed, beyond dismay,
Life's hardest truth,
"Nothing Gold Can Stay".

Fleeting Moment

What can you say in a moment?
When the heart shatters, you cannot stop it from
breaking
We try to console but
What do you say in a moment
When pure silence and hope pass overhead,
forgotten
Tell me, What do I say in a moment,
When the moment is fleeting?

It Comes

It comes when we are ready,

It comes when we are not,

It comes for those in plenty,

It comes regardless of lot.

It comes for all ages, races, and sex,

It comes and hurts those who care,

It comes without knowing,

Though we know it is there–

It comes in times of darkness,

It comes in times of light,

It comes whether it's wrong or if it's right,

It's timing is always variable,

Just know it's always there,

For it comes just as planned, when you are met
with Death's cold stare.

Suicide

Your face is peaceful now,
I cannot see the flashes of fear in your eyes,
However, they are closed now never to open
again,
No, not in this world.

It was then I realized,
How quickly the human life can impact,
You, now a face that haunts my darkest dreams,
A person who makes me reconsider my words,
Before releasing them into the void,
Never to be retracted.

While perhaps I was a sliver of hope,
A glimmer of faith, in those last hours,
You gave me a never-ending nightmare,
If only we could have known.

For Frost

Two options presented fire and ice
In the end, you're right
both would suffice.
A human world hell-bent on our desires
Would surely end our lives in fire
The cold ice of hate is also harsh
With potential to freeze us once it starts.

Desire will consume until there's nothing left to
burn
While Dante fears that ice, brings about our
demise.

Two equal matches faced
Desire and Hate
Is what will bring about humanity's fate
What the end brings Frost, I don't know
But if I had to choose
Surely, it's both.

Starry Night

I look up at your night sky
And wonder what you
Saw here that influenced you
To paint the picture that in
No way matches the true sky.

I look at your painting the deep strokes,
From painting with the wrong end of the brush
Or is that why you did it?

An act of defiance, an in-your-face
Challenge to art, nature, reality
Representing the real, unnaturally
Showing us beautiful chaos like you loved to do
Probing the inner chaos we attempt to hide,
Bringing it to the surface..